discovermore
Your Government

The Judicial Branch

Ezra E. Knopp

Britannica®
Educational Publishing

IN ASSOCIATION WITH

R THE ROSEN PUBLISHING GROUP

Published in 2024 by Britannica Educational Publishing (a trademark of Encyclopædia Britannica, Inc.) in association with The Rosen Publishing Group, Inc.
2544 Clinton Street, Buffalo, NY 14224

Distributed exclusively by Rosen Publishing.
To see additional Britannica Educational Publishing titles, go to rosenpublishing.com.

Editor: Caitie McAneney
Book Design: Rachel Rising

Photo Credits: Cover; (series background) Dai Yim/Shutterstock.com; Cover, Orhan Cam/Shutterstock.com; p. 4 PeskyMonkey/Shutterstock.com; p. 5 https://commons.wikimedia.org/wiki/File:Supreme_Court_of_the_United_States_-_Roberts_Court_2022.jpg; p. 6 https://commons.wikimedia.org/wiki/File:P20220408AS-1584_(52068966295).jpg; p. 7 https://commons.wikimedia.org/wiki/File:Barack_Obama_and_Joe_Biden_with_Judge_Sonia_Sotomayor.jpg; p. 8 Felix Lipov/Shutterstock.com; p. 9 Mark Van Scyoc/Shutterstock.com; p. 10 https://commons.wikimedia.org/wiki/File:Official_roberts_CJ.jpg; p. 11 LouiesWorld1/Shutterstock.com; p. 12 https://commons.wikimedia.org/wiki/File:Library_of_the_Supreme_Court_of_the_United_States,_Washington,_D.C._-_August,_2015.jpg; p. 13 Wang Sing/Shutterstock.com; p. 15 https://commons.wikimedia.org/wiki/File:Neil_Gorsuch_C80xEOPWAAARxOK.jpg; p. 15 https://commons.wikimedia.org/wiki/File:Sonia_Sotomayor_on_first_day_of_confirmation_hearings.jpg; p. 16 Prilutskiy/Shutterstock.com; p. 17 PENpics Studio/Shutterstock.com; p. 19 Gorodenkoff/Shutterstock.com; p. 19 mark reinstein/Shutterstock.com; p. 20 Georgios Kollidas/Shutterstock.com; p. 21 https://commons.wikimedia.org/wiki/File:Chief_Justice_John_Marshall.jpeg; p. 22 https://commons.wikimedia.org/wiki/File:Robert_F._Wagner_with_Little_Rock_students_NYWTS.jpg; p. 23 https://commons.wikimedia.org/wiki/File:Black-and-white-white-photography-usa-america-black-1142547.jpg; p. 24 https://commons.wikimedia.org/wiki/File:Thurgood-marshall-2.jpg; p. 25 https://commons.wikimedia.org/wiki/File:Thurgood_Marshall_and_President_Lyndon_B._Johnson_June_13,_1967_-_LBJ_Museum_C5706-1.jpg; p. 26 Rena Schild/Shutterstock.com; p. 27 https://commons.wikimedia.org/wiki/File:Ruth_Bader_Ginsburg.jpg; p. 29 corgarashu/ Shutterstock.com; p. 29 Bob Korn/ Shutterstock.com.

Cataloguing-in-Publication Data

Names: Knopp, Ezra E.
Title: The judicial branch / Ezra E. Knopp.
Description: New York : Britannica Educational Publishing, in Association with Rosen Educational Services. 2024. | Series: Discover more: your government | Includes glossary and index.
Identifiers: ISBN 9781642828993 (library bound) | ISBN 9781642828986 (pbk) | ISBN 9781642829006 (ebook)
Subjects: LCSH: Courts--United States--Juvenile literature.
Classification: LCC KF8720.K66 2024 | DDC 347.73'2–dc23

Manufactured in the United States of America

CPSIA Compliance Information: Batch #CSBRIT24. For further information contact Rosen Publishing at 1-800-237-9932.

Find us on

Contents

What Is the Judicial Branch?

The United States government was founded on the idea of liberty and justice for its citizens. A nation that values justice works to make sure people are treated fairly and laws are applied correctly to all.

Three branches make up the U.S. government: the legislative branch that makes laws, the executive branch that carries out laws, and the judicial branch that decides if laws are fair and followed. The judicial branch of the United States government is a system of courts. Sometimes people go to court when laws are broken. In other cases, courts make decisions about the laws themselves.

The Supreme Court works in Washington, D.C. The building reads "Equal justice under law."

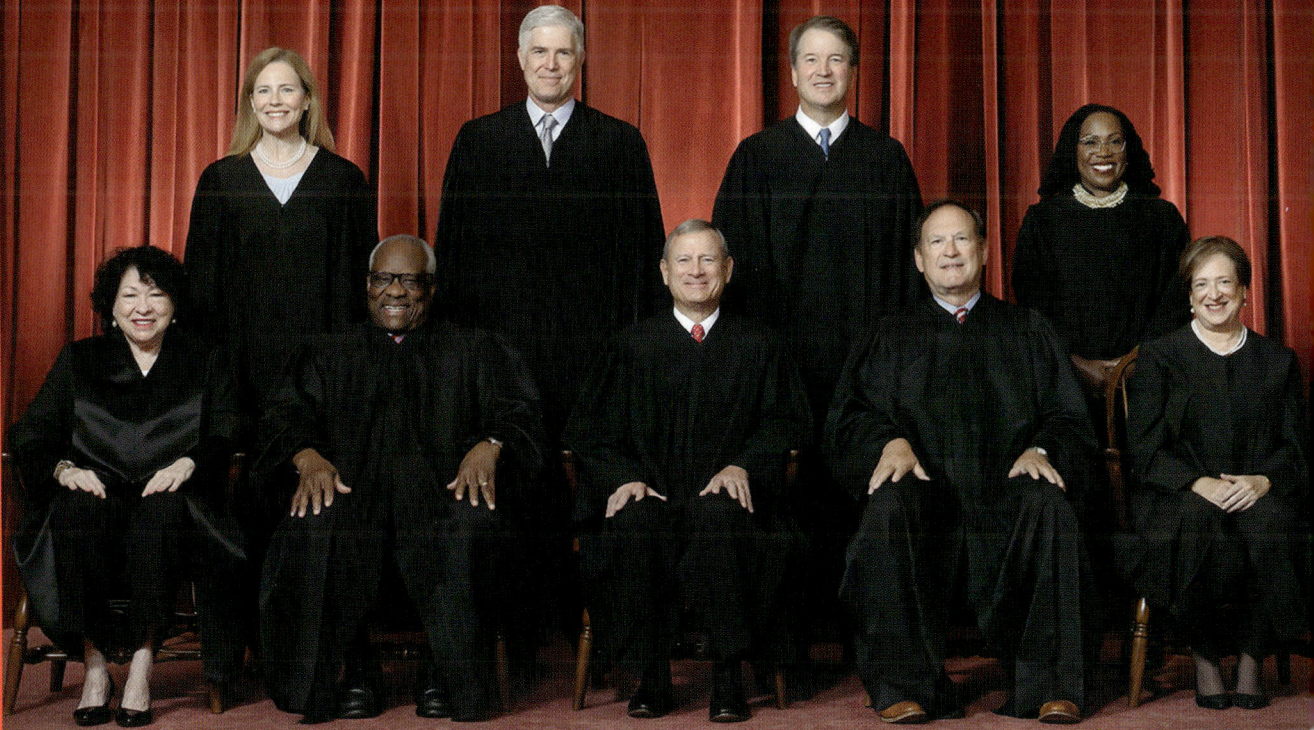

Each local government and state have their own judicial system. The federal court system is above that, handling legal cases that affect the **federal government**. The Supreme Court is the highest court in the nation.

WORD WISE
The federal government is the national government.

Understanding the Constitution

The U.S. Constitution is the foundation for the work the Supreme Court does. This document, used since 1787, organized the national government, set laws, and protected citizens' rights. The judicial branch uses the U.S. Constitution and other laws of the U.S. government to settle cases. It can also strike down a law passed by Congress if the Supreme Court declares that it goes against the Constitution. If the president makes an order that is unconstitutional, the Supreme Court can stop that, too.

President Joe Biden nominated Ketanji Brown Jackson to be the first Black woman on the Supreme Court in 2022.

President Barack Obama nominated Sonia Sotomayor as the first Hispanic person on the Supreme Court in 2009.

The legislative and executive branches have some power over the judicial branch. The president nominates, or proposes, all federal judges. The nominees then must be approved by the Senate. This nomination and approval process is important, especially for the Supreme Court since justices keep their jobs for life.

The Work of the Lower Courts

Imagine if the Supreme Court had to decide all of the cases that needed to be heard in the whole country. It wouldn't be possible! Therefore, the lower courts do much of the work of the judicial branch.

Judges in a court of appeals have the power to overturn, or undo, the judgments of the lower courts.

UNITED STATES COURT OF APPEALS

The Elijah Barrett Prettyman U.S. Courthouse in Washington, D.C., is home to the United States District Court for the District of Columbia and the United States Court of Appeals for the District of Columbia Circuit.

District courts are the lowest level of federal courts. There are 94 of these courts in the United States. These are separated into 12 groups, called circuits. A person who loses a case in a district court can appeal the decision in a court of appeals. There are 12 of these courts, one for each circuit. Panels, or groups, of judges usually hear cases in courts of appeals. The court of appeals usually has the last word on a case, though in some high-importance cases, it is reviewed by the Supreme Court.

WORD WISE

To appeal a case is to ask for a higher court to think about the case and make a new decision.

The Highest Court

Once a case goes through the lower courts and the court of appeals, it may eventually end up with the Supreme Court—the highest court in the nation. The nine judges on the Supreme Court are called justices. The leader is called the chief justice. The others are associate justices. When the justices decide a case, each person has an equal say. Some of their decisions are very close, with five members voting one way and four voting the other way.

The current chief justice of the Supreme Court is John G. Roberts. He was nominated by George W. Bush in 2005.

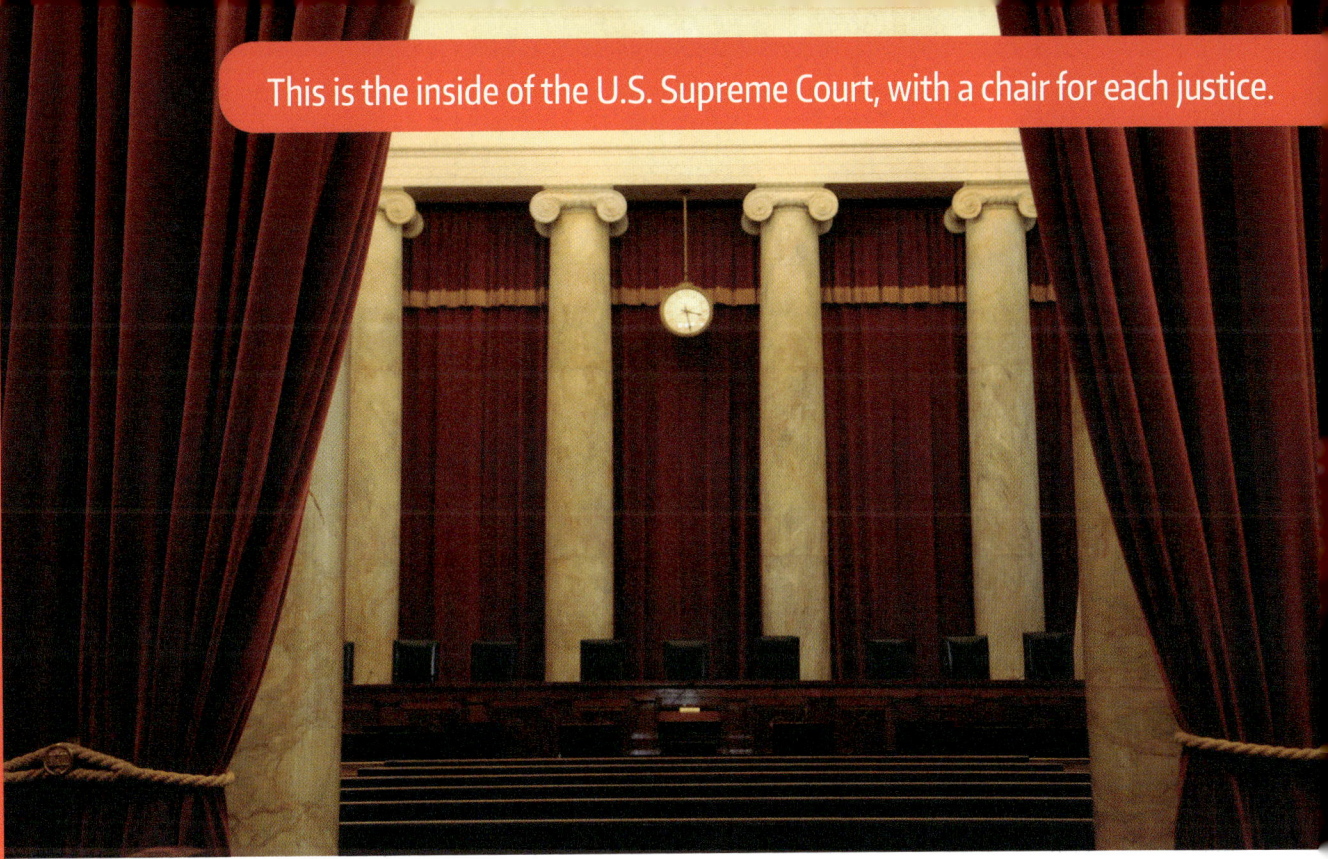

The Supreme Court meets in its own building. It is in Washington, D.C. The building is four stories tall. It has large columns at the front entrance. Built between 1931 and 1935, it is where all Supreme Court cases are decided.

Consider This

With nine justices on the Supreme Court, there's never a tie in a case. What would happen if there were an even number of justices?

When the justices aren't hearing a case, they may be working in their **chambers**. The Supreme Court building also has spaces for other people to work. A library is on the third floor. The court hears cases in the courtroom. This has a high desk where the justices sit. There are special seats for guests of the court as well.

This is the library of the Supreme Court.

Supreme Court sessions are open to the public. However, there aren't a lot of seats.

The justices need many people to help them run the court. They are called court officers. The court clerk keeps track of the calendars and schedules. The court marshal is responsible for security, as well as keeping the court on time. The marshal uses colored signals to tell lawyers when their time is up. The court also has librarians for research and resources.

WORD WISE
Chambers are the rooms where judges work.

A Presidential Nomination

All federal judges are nominated by the U.S. president. That gives presidents a lot of power to shape the courts. The president picks a person who has excellent knowledge of the law. Most presidents choose nominees who think like they do or whom they have worked with before.

After the president nominates a person, the Senate must approve that choice. First, a small group, called a committee, has a hearing. Committee members ask nominees about their thoughts on the law. After the committee votes on the nominee, the whole Senate votes. A nominee must gain at least 51 votes from the 100 senators to become a judge. Often, there's a lot of attention on Supreme Court nominations and approvals.

compare and contrast

How state court judges are selected varies from state to state. In some states, judges are elected. In others, the governor or a legislative committee appoints judges. What are the advantages of each system?

Justice Sonia Sotomayor smiles at her confirmation hearing in 2009.

Different Kinds of Cases

What kinds of cases are tried before federal courts? In these courts, you'll see cases that deal with whether a law is permitted by the Constitution and disputes between states. Federal courts also hear all **bankruptcy** cases.

Family law cases, such as those about divorces and adoptions, also take place in state courts.

When a company goes bankrupt, the business is closed.

Federal and state courts follow many of the same rules and procedures. But different cases are tried in state courts, such as most criminal cases. State courts deal with personal injury cases, as well as with cases involving the wills of people who have died. The ruling of a state trial court can be appealed to a higher state court. After that, it may move to the U.S. Supreme Court if necessary.

WORD WISE

People or businesses that are deep in debt can declare bankruptcy to get a fresh start.

Listening and Deciding

In the lower courts, juries decide some cases and judges decide others. During a trial, jury members listen carefully to the arguments that each side's lawyers make. Then the jury discusses the case in private until all of the members agree on a decision in the case.

In Supreme Court cases, there are no witnesses and there is no jury. After lawyers for both sides make their arguments, the justices meet in private to make a decision. A majority of the justices must agree before the court can make its decision.

One justice writes a statement called an opinion to explain the decision. Justices who disagree with the decision can write their own opinions, which are called dissenting opinions. The outcomes of these cases are often used to decide cases in the lower courts.

Justice Ruth Bader Ginsburg was known for her strong dissents.

compareandcontrast

Supreme Court justices can disagree when the court makes a decision. People on a jury must all agree on a decision. What are the advantages of each method?

In lower court cases, juries are chosen to listen to a case and make a decision about it.

19

Landmark Cases

The Supreme Court has heard many thousands of cases in its history. The most important ones are called landmark cases. The decisions that came from these cases changed American history.

Thomas Jefferson was president during the *Marbury v. Madison* case.

One famous example of a landmark case is *Marbury v. Madison,* a case from 1803. The Constitution does not explain how to determine if a law that Congress has passed goes against the Constitution. Chief Justice John Marshall's decision in *Marbury v. Madison* stated that this is the Supreme Court's job. It set a **precedent** that the Supreme Court would decide whether laws were constitutional or not. Called judicial review, this gave the Supreme Court more power than it had before.

WORD WISE

A precedent sets an example for how things will be done in the future.

At one time in U.S. history, segregation was legal. Segregation was the forced separation of Black and white people in public places. This was allowed under the 1896 *Plessy v. Ferguson* Supreme Court decision. In the case, Homer Plessy was part white and part black. Plessy was arrested when he refused to ride in a train car set aside for African Americans. He appealed his case all the way to the Supreme Court. Plessy argued that separate cars for African Americans and whites were unconstitutional. The court disagreed with him.

In 1957, these nine Black students entered a formerly all-white school in Little Rock, Arkansas. They faced shouts and threats from an angry mob.

The *Plessy v. Ferguson* decision made "separate but equal" okay under the law. That meant Black people had to use different schools, restrooms, and even drinking fountains.

A later court reversed that decision. It decided that segregation was wrong. In *Brown v. Board of Education of Topeka* (1954), it ruled that having separate schools for white and African American children was unconstitutional. This set a precedent, and in the following years, other courts ruled against similar unfair laws too.

Consider This

Brown v. Board of Education of Topeka reversed the decision the Supreme Court made in *Plessy v. Ferguson*. Is it a good idea for the government to admit when it is wrong and change its mind?

Famous Justices

Over a hundred Supreme Court Justices have served on the country's highest court since its beginning. Some of them have become famous for their work. One is John Marshall. Marshall was the fourth chief justice of the Supreme Court. He served for 34 years, longer than anyone else. Before joining the court, he had served in his state legislature, in Congress, and as **secretary of state**. His first important case was *Marbury v. Madison.*

Thurgood Marshall made his mark as both a lawyer and a Supreme Court justice.

President Lydon B. Johnson nominated Thurgood Marshall to the Supreme Court.

Thurgood Marshall was the first African American justice on the Supreme Court. Before he was on the court, he argued cases before the court as a lawyer. His early work included his winning argument in the case of *Brown v. Board of Education of Topeka*. Appointed to the Supreme Court in 1967, he was a strong supporter of equal rights for all U.S. citizens.

WORD WISE

The secretary of state helps the president deal with foreign countries.

Sandra Day O'Connor became the first female Supreme Court justice in 1981. Very few women were lawyers or judges when she graduated from law school. She worked her way up in government. She served as a lawmaker and a judge in Arizona. Later in life, she wrote books, including a history of the Supreme Court.

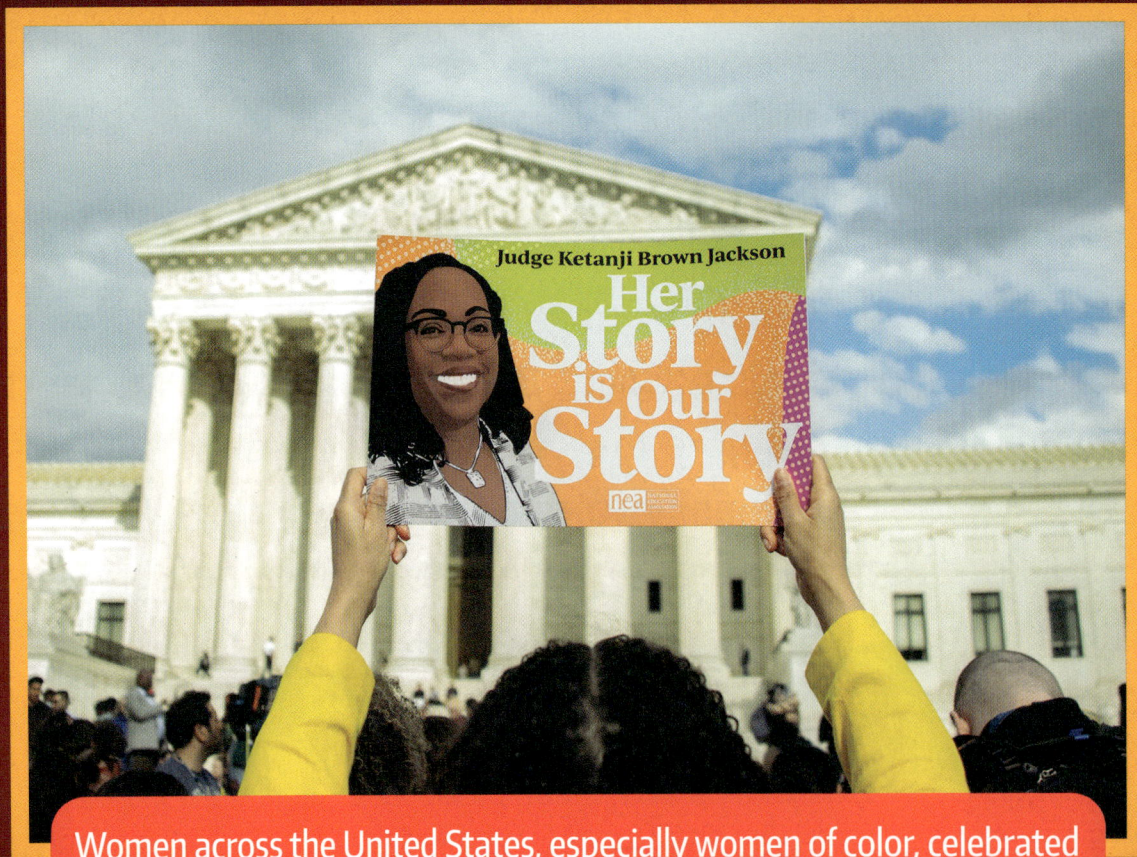

Women across the United States, especially women of color, celebrated Ketanji Brown Jackson's confirmation to the Supreme Court.

Ruth Bader Ginsburg was the second woman on the Supreme Court. She was a strong fighter for women's rights.

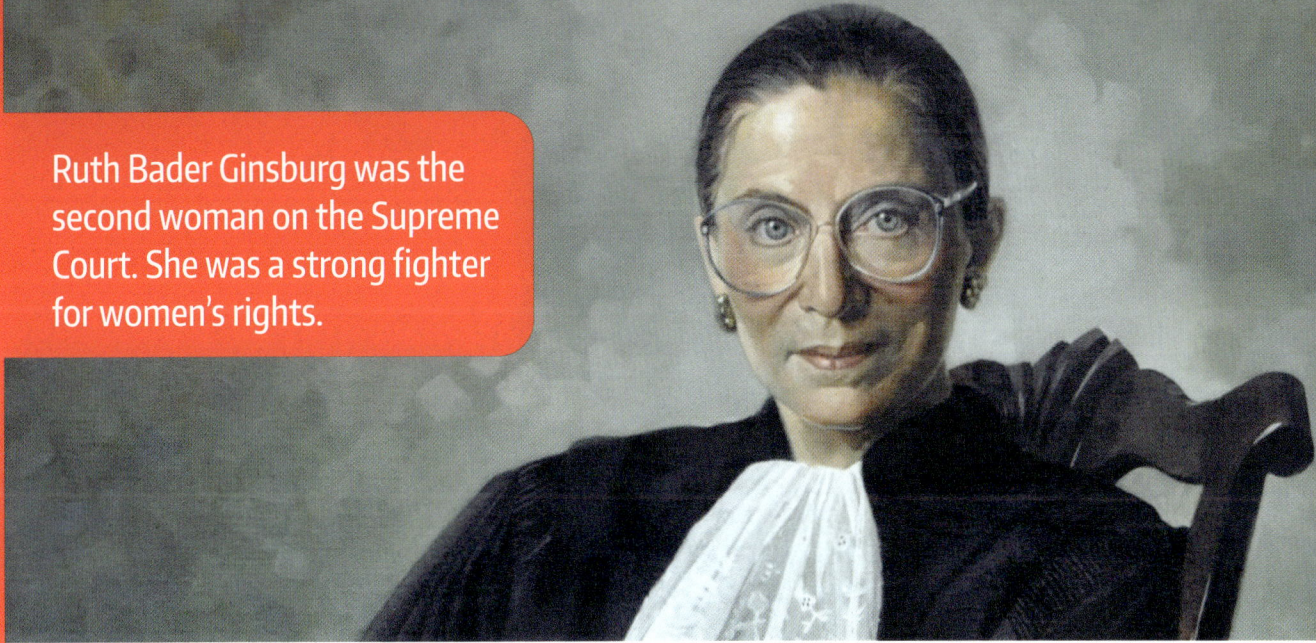

Sonia Sotomayor is the first Hispanic justice, as well as the third woman, to serve on the Supreme Court. She had been a district-court judge in New York. Later, she became a judge for an appeals court. She was confirmed as a justice in 2009.

In 2022, Ketanji Brown Jackson became the first Black woman on the Supreme Court. Before that, she had worked on the U.S. District Court for the District of Columbia.

Consider This

Over time, the Supreme Court has become more diverse. Why is that important for justice?

Justice for All

Every year, the Supreme Court is asked to review about 7,000 cases. They choose between 100 to 150 cases to hear. These cases often cover important issues that will affect every American. While the decisions of lower courts may not have the same sweeping impact, they have a huge effect on the lives of the people involved in each case.

The judicial branch has a duty to make sure people are being treated fairly in the United States. It must make sure that anybody who is accused of a crime gets a fair trial. Making sure laws follow the Constitution and settling disputes between people fairly are both important jobs of this branch of government. The judicial branch serves the country by following the Constitution and ensuring justice for all.

People often protest outside the Supreme Court building when something is important to them.

PROTECT LGBTQ+ WORKERS

PEOPLE FOR THE AMERICAN WAY

compare and contrast

Compare and contrast the roles of the lower courts and the Supreme Court. How are they the same and different?

One symbol, or sign, of justice is the balance, or scales. It stands for weighing facts and evidence, or proof, to make a fair decision.

Glossary

appoints: Officially names.

confirmed: Approved.

criminal: Having to do with things that are against the law.

disputes: Disagreements about matters.

diverse: Made up of things or people who are different from each other.

document: An official paper relied on as the basis, proof, or support of something.

elected: Voted into office.

jury: A group of people who make a decision in a legal case.

justice: Fair treatment, in particular fair treatment under the law.

landmark: A development that marks a turning point.

majority: A number greater than half.

nominates: Chooses someone for a job, position, office, or so forth.

opinion: A formal statement by a judge or court, explaining the reasons a decision was made according to the law.

rights: Things that a person is or should be morally or legally allowed to have, get, or do.

ruling: An official decision made by a judge or other authority.

trial: The hearing of a case in court.

witnesses: People who make statements in court about what they know or have seen.

For More Information

Books

Ahrens, Niki. *Sonia Sotomayor: First Latina Supreme Court Justice.* Minneapolis, MN: Lerner Publishing Group, 2022.

Charles, Tami. *Ketanji Brown Jackson: A Justice for All.* New York, NY: Simon & Schuster Books for Young Readers, 2023.

Tolli, Jenna. *Inside the Supreme Court.* New York, NY: Rosen Publishing, 2021.

Websites

Judicial Branch: The Supreme Court
www.ducksters.com/history/us_judicial_branch.php
Discover more facts about the U.S. Supreme Court.

The Nation's Court
www.timeforkids.com/k1/nations-court/
Take a look inside the U.S. Supreme Court.

Publisher's note to educators and parents: Our editors have carefully reviewed these websites to ensure that they are suitable for students. Many websites change frequently, however, and we cannot guarantee that a site's future contents will continue to meet our high standards of quality and educational value. Be advised that students should be closely supervised whenever they access the internet.

Index